How to Write
Great Dialog

Third Edition

James R. Callan

How to Write Great Dialog

James R. Callan.

For information, contact the author through his website, www.jamesrcallan.com.

How to Write Great Dialog

Third Edition, September 2021

Acknowledgements

Thank you to those who have encouraged me to write this book. I would not have undertaken this task without your support. I also want to send a special thanks to Lesley Diehl, Gay Ingram, Galand Nuchols, and Paul Paris for their insightful comments on the ideas, examples and exercises in this book. While any mistakes or shortcomings are entirely mine, these early readers made many helpful suggestions on how I might improve the effectiveness of the book. Thank you.

Contents

Chapter 1

Dialog: She Said; He Said

What are we talking about here?

Webster defines dialog as a talking together, conversation. Or, a written work in the form of a conversation, or the passage of talk in a book or play or radio.

Today, some might also include as dialog text messages between two or more people's telephones, or even messages sent via email. If you're writing an epistolary novel, one interpretation could mean the entire book.

However, as these forms may include various documents such as news clippings, diary entries, etc., for this book, we will limit our discussions to the more traditional meaning of dialog.

So what's the big deal? We all talk, carry on conversations–that's what Webster said: conversation. We can just record what people say, or we can imagine what they say, and write it down.

Recently, an article on the Internet said writing dialog is not as hard as you think. Go to some crowded spot and just listen for a couple of hours. Then, grab your computer and enter some of the stuff people were saying. It's that simple.

Wrong.

That sounds good, and I wish it were so. But it isn't. I'll discuss why in a few minutes.

First, though, let's settle one area of disagreement: how do you spell it. The dictionary lists both "dialog" and "dialogue" as correct spelling for the word. I will use dialog. For those who are convinced it should be only the longer form, please bear with me. You can chalk it up to my long years in mathematics where one often strove to reduce things to their simplest form.

Dialog for writers is a whole different story. To begin with, we talk about three kinds of dialog. No, that's not whispering, talking and screaming. The three types of dialog are **regular dialog, summary dialog,** and **internal dialog.** We will discuss those in chapters 6, 7, and 8.

For now, let me just say that dialog for the writer is much different than the dialog you hear in the office, on the street, in the grocery store, or eavesdropping at church. Yes, you hear dialog every day. But you can't just transcribe that and put it in a book. Not if you want to sell the book. So, in chapter 5, we'll explain how the writer's dialog is different from what you hear and participate in every day.

But to begin, let's see how dialog fits into the big picture.

Chapter 2

The Big 3

No, we're not talking about Grisham, Baldacci, and Roberts. We're talking about plot, character, and dialog.

Plot is the engine of a book. It's what makes the story move along. Without a decent plot, the reader is likely to say, "Nothing's happening. It's like watching water evaporate." Or, "Something is happening, but I will be old and grey before I can see any movement." Many books are plot driven. The action is the main thing. Most thriller books fall into this category. Yes, there are some characters in these, but plot is king.

Character is the heartbeat of the novel. It's what makes people care about the book. Character is why we have a book series. People who can't wait for the next book in a series to be published have developed a relationship with one of the characters, usually the protagonist. In *Character: The Heartbeat of the Novel* (Oak Tree Press, 2013, Third Edition 2021) the statement is made that when people say they loved a book, if you pin them down, it's a character in the book that they loved.

Dialog is what makes the book real. It is also, sadly, one of the reasons manuscripts are turned down. If the dialog doesn't read smoothly, doesn't do the things we say in the next chapter it *must* do, the manuscript is likely to get dumped.

Certainly there are other aspects of the novel, for example, setting. Many writers consider setting as another character. Some will even write a character sketch or character bio for setting. But the main point here is, if you get the Big 3 right, you are going to see your novel in print. It's that simple.

Am I making the job of writing a novel seem trivial? Not at all. It isn't a walk in the park to get the Big 3 done well. Many people, and many published authors, can get one or two of those expertly written into their book. Don't settle for that. Don't say, "Two out of three ain't bad." And never say, "It's in print. Who cares if I missed one of the Big 3?" You should care. Strive to get each of the Big 3 in your book at the highest degree of excellence you can achieve.

So, what is the purpose of dialog? Chapter 3 is devoted to explaining what dialog *should* do, and chapter 4 shows what it *can* do. It is amazing how much dialog can accomplish. The late Elmore Leonard, a master at dialog, was quoted as saying at a conference that "you can do everything with dialog." (He probably said dialogue.)

Before we get into all the things you can do with dialog, let's answer a question often asked by beginning writers. "How much dialog should I have?"

That's about like asking how long is a piece of rope. For rope, it is best to have as much as you need for the job, and not a lot more. Too much rope gets in the way, makes it harder to tie the knots, requires a knife to trim it down.

Same thing with dialog. You need as much as you need to get the job done, and no more. Too much dialog, like too much rope, gets in the way. The reader is likely to ask what the author was doing. Was he getting paid by the word? Or maybe the reader will just skip over it—never a good thing. You don't want the reader to bypass any sentence you have written.

Why?

It means you're not keeping her interest. Her mind is wandering. You are losing the reader.

Also like the rope, too much dialog makes it harder to tie up the loose ends. It's like the old saying during World War II: "Loose lips sink ships." Here, loose dialog sinks novels.

And lastly, too much dialog means you need to trim it down. As one famous writer said (and I'm paraphrasing), I write the book, then go back and cut out all the parts the reader will likely skip. For many writers, what needs to get cut is dialog that is not necessary.

Let's go look at the purpose of dialog and what it **must** do.

Chapter 3

To What End?

"And what is the use of a book," thought Alice, "without pictures or conversations?" (From Alice in Wonderland.)

Since we are not talking about picture books today, we might adjust Alice's quote to ask what good is a book without dialog. Certainly there have been books without dialog, but they are few and far between and not many of those are ranked amongst the great books.

It is generally agreed that **dialog must either further the plot, or help define the characters.** One good line of dialog can set the plot. One good line of dialog can define a character. The key words are, "good line." Let me give an example where dialog helps define the plot.

Example: Hunter was being held in a secure government prison. Without explanation, he is turned loose. A friend picks him up and asks, "Why'd they let you out?"

Hunter replies, "The only reason I can come up with is, they want to use me as bait."

The reader may or may not realize at this point that the bulk of the book will be about Hunter being the hunted, for indeed, he is put out as bait to entice a rival group to come out of hiding and attack Hunter, thus exposing itself.

Example: In *The Silver Medallion*, Crystal has asked Juan Grande to help her rescue two young girls being held slaves by a ruthless man and his men. Juan Grande says he and some friends will attempt to get the girls out, but it is too dangerous for Crystal to go. Crystal tenses her muscles, trying to keep from shaking.

"I'm terrified. But I ask for your help and I cannot let you take all the risks while I sit back here in safety."

Immediately, the reader knows several important things about Crystal. She is not some adventure-loving super woman. She is an ordinary person and rightfully afraid. But she came to rescue the girls and even as she shakes with fear, she insists on sharing the risks. The reader sees what Crystal is made of, sees her resolve, sees how dedicated she is to saving the young girls.

You could *tell* the reader all this. But these twenty-four words of dialog *show* the reader much better, much more clearly, and much more convincingly. These are Crystal's words, Crystal's feelings. These two sentences of dialog help define the character.

Those two goals—further the plot and help define the characters—are very important and you should keep that in mind as you craft dialog. For each section of dialog, ask yourself, "Does this further the plot? Does it help define the characters?" If you can't answer yes to one of those, you might want to reconsider the piece of dialog. Improve it or cut it.

However, dialog can do much, much more. After you do the following exercises, read the next chapter to see other things that dialog is capable of doing.

Exercises

1. Craft a small piece of dialog that helps set the plot. You can use a book you read recently and see if you can help define the plot in dialog.

2. Craft a small piece of dialog that foreshadows the plot. This is very similar to exercise 1 above, but whereas exercise 1 points directly to the main plot point, this reference is more subtle, giving a small hint to the plot.

3. Take a character from your book. Write a line or two of dialog (spoken by the character) which helps define this character. You can use the protagonist, antagonist, or the protagonist's sidekick. (You can use some other character, but those three are often the easiest.) Try to do this in one sentence, or two short sentences.

4. Take a different character (whom we'll call B for this exercise) and write a few lines of dialog spoken by another character who is talking about B.

Chapter 4

Added Attractions

While I'm not backing away from the statement that dialog should advance the plot or help define the characters, it is capable of doing so much more. The words convey some information to the reader, but the way you craft the dialog can provide added benefits. It can send this information in such a way that the reader doesn't perceive she is getting extra information. And it can deliver this information or feeling in a much more powerful way, a much more believable way.

In Chapter 2, I attributed to Elmore Leonard, a master at dialog, the statement that you can do everything with dialog. Let's look at some of the things dialog can do for you, the writer.

Dialog can set the **scene**. Now I know you generally think of setting the scene with description and that's fine. But dialog can do it, sometimes even better.

Example: "Are we really going to do this?" Fran's forehead wrinkled and two vertical lines formed between her eyebrows.

"Yes we are. We walk right in like we belong there." She slid the card she had recovered from the dead man's pocket into the slot and the door clicked open. "Let's go. Look confident."

They stepped in and closed the door behind them. A sharp click told them it had locked.

"Oh my." A frown crept up Joan's face.

"Oh my is right," whispered Fran. "And right now, I'm not thinking so much about the statue as how can we get out of this smoke-filled dungeon alive."

"This could be the United Nations. I've never seen so many different nationalities in one place."

"Yeah, the UN of thugs. Do you see anyone you think is not wanted by Interpol or the CIA or the FBI."

"That looks like a bar over there. I could sure use a drink about now," Joan said. "A stiff one."

"It's so smoky I can barely ... Did you see that? That Japanese man just opened his briefcase and ... and it's filled with money."

"Just like in the movies."

"And somebody always gets killed in the movies."

We've set the scene with dialog. We have told the reader what the place looked like. Even here, we've just hinted at it, left a lot to the reader's imagination. The two women have told us about the characters in the room and given us a little bit of the feel. We know there are many nationalities and the characters appear shady. We know there is a great deal of money involved. And we get a sense of danger. Is it also furthering the plot? Yes is it. So we're meeting the admonition that dialog should further the plot, but we are getting another benefit. We're setting the scene.

We could also provide the **setting and location** via dialog.

Example: "I love Puerto Vallarta in July. You will, too."

Gail twirled the umbrella, causing rain drops to fly off in all directions.

"Stop that. You're getting me all wet," said Marie.

"The days are bright, clear. Then, around seven in the evening, you will get a great rain. And tomorrow, another bright blue sky. What's not to like?"

Dialog can also provide **foreshadowing**. We saw a little of that in a previous example. Here's another.

Example: Jill's eyebrows shot up. "You're really going to do that?"

"You bet your favorite earrings I am."

"Not me. You wouldn't catch me within a mile of that place."

With just a few words of dialog, we have set the scene for Jill to go to this terrible place, whatever it is. She says she'd never go there and the astute reader knows poor Jill will wind up there. Yes, you're right. That dialog is also furthering the plot. That's good. It's furthering the plot *and* foreshadowing. Two for the price of one, all in dialog.

There is probably no better way to show the **relationship** between two characters than using dialog.

Example: "I see you couldn't stay away," said Wilson.

"I wouldn't have missed it – if only to see you sweat."

"I may disappoint you."

"No. You'll sweat like a pig. And in the end, I expect you'll commit perjury."

I don't have to tell you there is no love lost between these two. They told you that without ever saying how they felt about one another. Here, dialog is not only helping define the characters (meeting one of the requirements), it is also showing the relationship between two characters.

Of course, dialog is a good place to **describe a character** in many ways.

Example: “I don’t know who it was, but it wasn’t Bob. He’s so straight forward, so honest, he wouldn’t even understand what was going on.”

We could tell you a lot about Bob in a paragraph of description. But here, with just a few words of dialog, we’ve given the reader the essence of Bob.

Example: In my book *A Ton of Gold*, the old, western sheriff says to Crystal.

“You look like you been rode hard and put up wet.”

I didn’t need any other description of how Crystal looked. The sheriff’s one short sentence of dialog tells us.

An important aspect of any novel, be it romance, mystery, western, fantasy, whatever, is **conflict**. There are many who say there should be conflict on every page. I would adjust that just a little and say **conflict or tension (or its synonym stress)** on every page. But how do you get conflict or tension on every page? Dialog offers a great opportunity. I’m going to talk more about this in chapter 10, but it’s so important, I’ll just give a little foreshadowing here.

Example: “You sound different today.”

“No I don’t.”

There's conflict, in seven words.

Let's look at how dialog can create **tension**, a very vital aspect in any novel. While similar to conflict, it's different. Tension means a strain has been created. That can be a strain on one person, remembering something, or seeing something that causes unpleasant feelings.

Example: Sandra glanced across the street. There was Ralph. *What is he doing here? Is he going to try to destroy my life again?*

It could mean a strain has been created between the two people in the dialog, not enough to be called a conflict, but building a little tension.

Example: "Who is that person we just made a point of avoiding?" asked Wanda.

"He's the man who tried to destroy my life." Sandra closed her eyes and tried to quiet her nerves. "I know he's going to try again."

Or both participants in the dialog can add to the tension.

Example: "What did that man say to you?"

"Nothing. Don't worry about it."

"No. He seemed to upset you. What did he say?"

"Drop it."

Now we have a little tension between these two friends. It's not a real conflict, but a little strain has been created between them. How much tension? How much do you want?

It depends on the next line.

If indeed she does drop it, then we have that mild tension. But what if she pursues it? Depending on how hard she pushes, you can ramp the tension to whatever level you want it, and right into conflict – all in dialog.

If **stress** comes to your mind more easily than tension, you can just replace the word "tension" in the discussion above with the word "stress.

Keep in mind, under enough stress, a person may let words slip out of their mouth they would never say normally. Or they may disclose something, perhaps feelings, that would be kept secret if they were not under tension.

As little as one line of dialog can make us **like or dislike a character**.

Example: Lily Underjohn hugged the small dog close to her neck. "Oh, Melissa, have you met my darling little cutie-pie Miss Prissy?" She held the dog out so Melissa could get a closer look.

"That ugly mutt? Should have been fed to a tiger." Melissa was not smiling.

We may wonder about Lily, but there's no doubt about Melissa. Mean spirited. And we immediately don't like her, even if we're not fond of Lily and her dog.

And just as easily, we can make the reader like a character through dialog.

Example: It wasn't her concern, but at that moment she knew she couldn't walk away.

"Mr. Johnson, you shouldn't treat the boy that way. He's trying to do his best. But you and I know he has to overcome a handicap that others in the class don't have. I know you're busy. Would you like for me to give him a little extra help?"

It isn't her duty, but she's willing not only to supply some extra help, but also to confront Mr. Johnson. Notice, she softens it by saying she knows he is busy. So is she, but she'll give the young boy some help.

Naturally, a longer sequence of dialog can present an even better opportunity to enhance this feeling toward a character, either like or dislike. However, sometimes, a well crafted single line can have an immediate and powerful effect on the reader.

As you can see, dialog can do a lot, even while satisfying the initial requirements of either furthering the plot or helping define a character.

Dialog is an excellent way to control the **pace** of the novel. Use short, quick dialog to quicken the pace of the novel. Use slower, methodical, even rambling conversations to slow the pace.

Example: "When?"
"Now."
"Now?"
"Right now."
"But—."
"No buts. Move it."

We're moving the pace as well. Done properly, the reader will actually speed up her reading.

On the other hand, you can slow the pace when it's been moving fast and the reader needs a little break.

Example: "I can't believe what a beautiful day this has turned out to be. That little burst of rain just washed everything clean. Look at that sky."

"I am. Plus, the rain cooled things. Let's just stroll through the park. I'm in no hurry. Are you?"

"Not in the least."

"Good. We can catch a taxi on the other side. This is too nice to pass up."

Again, the conversation will actually slow the reader, slow the pace of the novel, gain the feeling you want the reader to have right now, before the big scene.

But, there are also things that dialog should **NOT** do.

Do not use dialog to tell a character things he already knows, just because you want to get that information over to the reader. The reader will ask, "Why is Joan telling Gladys that? Gladys already knows it." Find another way to deliver the information.

Example: "As you know, Max, mother had two other husbands after our father died. The first one, Randolph, moved in when we were teenagers. He was mean to Mother and to us, and he took our car one day and drove off and never returned."

You've already said, "As you know." So, don't tell him. Unless you've established that Max doesn't remember anything, or is mentally deficient, he already knows this. He was there as a teenager. If you need to get this information to the reader, find another way. This is phony and the reader will recognize it as such.

You should not use dialog to express the *author's* views. You're writing fiction, not an editorial. Whatever views you want to impart, do not do it as dialog in your novel. You can certainly create a character who might share your views and that character could legitimately espouse such views. But even here, use caution. The novel is to entertain. It is not meant to be a podium for the author.

Golden and Good in a Novel

Example:

No. That's not a mistake – well, not completely. I wanted to emphasize that sometimes silence is not only golden but can say more than a dozen words. Let me fill in a better example.

Example: "They're coming tonight," Will said. "I'm going to need your help."

Buck drew his lips into a thin, straight line, but said nothing.

The seconds passed.

Then, Buck turned and walked away.

Or in a romance –

Example: "I love you, Mark."

He put the car in drive and eased out of the parking lot. Silence and sorrow filled the car on the long drive to her house.

Another thought on improving your dialog

If you are not trying to tell us something about a character, try to avoid the stilted expressions in the left column below. Use the shorter version given in the right column.

Apart from the fact that	Except
At this point in time	Now
Because of the fact	Because
Due to the fact that	Due to
By means of	By
During the course of	During
Except for the fact that	Except
Irrespective of the fact that	Despite
Subsequent to	After
To the best of my knowledge	I believe
In the recent past	Recently
In all probability	Probably
In order to	To

You have seen what dialog must do, what dialog can do and what dialog shouldn't do. In the next chapter, we'll talk about how to craft good dialog. But first, here are a few exercises to reinforce some of the ideas in this chapter.

Exercises

1. Go back and read the example of dialog used to set the scene. Then write a little piece of dialog that will set a different scene for the reader. This could be a scene in your work in progress, or you can just invent a scene and use dialog to set it up.

2. Write a sentence or two of dialog that gives the reader the location of the scene.

3. Write a short piece of dialog that gives the reader, not just the location, but a feeling for the location where this scene takes place.

4. Go back and read the example of dialog used for foreshadowing. Then write a piece of dialog that foreshadows a coming event. This event can be the main problem for the protagonist, or it may be a smaller problem.

5. Write a short piece of dialog between two characters that shows the reader the relationship, good or bad, between the participants in the dialog.

6. Write a piece of dialog that will make the reader immediately like a character.

7. Okay, how about a piece of dialog that will make the reader dislike one of the participants in the dialog.

8. Write a piece of dialog that will create tension.

9. Write a piece of dialog where silence plays an important part.

10. Find a section of dialog in one of your manuscripts where you have relied on adverbs. See if you can find stronger verbs and eliminate the adverbs.

Chapter 5

Natural vs. Novel Dialog

What's the big deal on dialog? We all engage in dialog every day. If we want natural dialog for our book, we can get that just listening to ourselves talk with friends. Right?

Wrong.

Natural dialog tends to wander, to be redundant, to include a lot of filler words, pleasantries, meaningless comments.

"Hi. How are you?"

"I'm fine. How about you?"

"I'm doing okay. How's the family?"

"They're all doing well. How are Mary and the twins?"

"All doing good."

"Glad to hear that."

"I wanted to ask you about that bomb threat."

Oh! We've finally gotten to the point of this conversation.

Don't do that unless you want to make the point that the first speaker is deliberately delaying getting to the meat of the conversation, the reason he has made a point to talk with the second person.

Novel dialog, unlike natural dialog which may wander around before getting to the heart of the conversation, must be to the point—lean, terse, free of superfluous words—and should flow smoothly.

That's worth repeating. As a rule, novel dialog must be lean and free of superfluous words.

Court transcripts capture exactly what is said—and are incredible boring. You would like dialog that produces sparks, at least part of the time.

Certain circumstances may call for the dialog to lag, to be rough, to show indecision, or uncertainty. You may want to convey to the reader the state of mind of the speaker. But you should allow this into dialog *only* with a conscious decision. Even in this situation, first consider the possibility that a few words might convey that state of mind without going through the dialog necessary to get the same feeling.

Let's look at an example of natural dialog and then how the same dialog, the same ideas, might be written in a novel.

Example of natural dialog:

"Hey, Michael. Long time no see."

"You're right there."

"How long's it been?"

"I'm not sure. Maybe nine months. How's Mary?"

"Doing good."

"And the kids?"

"Eatin' and growin' and gettin' into trouble."

"That's teenagers for you."

"Yeah. Joey's fourteen and Mira's fift – no – sixteen now. Don't know which one's the most trouble."

"I guess it depends on the day."

"How ya doing?"

"Everything's fine. How about you?"

"Not good."

"Sorry to hear that. I guess we all have our up days and our down days."

"Sure got a downer right now. Got me a serious problem."

"I'm not surprised, Joe. What is your problem?"

"Need a thousand bucks? Like today."

And in the novel:

"Hey, Michael. Been awhile. How ya doing?"

"I'm doing well. What do you need?"

Joe looked down at his feet, then back up to Michael's chin. "Need a thousand bucks. Like today."

The natural dialog runs 112 words, most of it unnecessary. The novel version is only thirty words, and twelve of those are describing Joe's unease. So, it's really 112 vs. 18. It's clear Michael knows that Joe wants something, so he cuts right to the problem. This moves the story along much faster than the natural dialog does. It avoids the possibility of the reader thinking, "Get on with the story. I don't care about the kids and that other stuff." Of course, if the kids play a role in the plot, then perhaps that part could be left in. If not, cut it out.

Those five words apply to dialog throughout your manuscript. So, let's make it a rule.

Rule #1 –Not necessary? Cut it out.

No fillers. You are not being paid by the word. Be ruthless in cutting out anything superfluous.

Dialog should either move the plot along, or reveal more about a character.

Pleasantries like, “How’s it going?” or, “It’s a beautiful day,” or, “Hi. How’re you doing?” have no place in novel dialog, unless it is important to the plot. If “How’s it going?” leads to the character giving us the real problem he’s facing, that is, the plot of the book, then it stays. Otherwise, cut it out. Unless “It’s a beautiful day” leads to something significant, cut it out.

By now, you’re getting the idea I think novel dialog should be spare, as in lean—no fat. Skinny. But, powerful. You want your dialog to exude power, and that means cut the fat.

“Hi, Mary. How’re you doing?”

“Good. And you?”

“Things are great.”

“Glad to hear that. Been to any good movies recently?”

“No. Too busy getting the kids ready for school.”

“Oh, it is getting close to that time of year, isn’t it.”

“Too close; too fast.”

“Isn’t that the truth.”

“Have you seen Joan lately? I’ve called and gone by and I never can catch her.”

This is a typical conversation between two women meeting at the post office. In fact, what the reader (and the plot) wants to get to is that Joan is missing. No one can find her. The novel dialog starts where we want to be. So, we salvage—

“Hi, Mary. Have you seen Joan lately? I’ve called and gone by and I never can catch her.”

I’ve put in all of the superfluous stuff, and then underlined the part that needs to be cut. You can see immediately that this second version—one line, eighteen words—gets right to the point, right to the place the reader wants to be. You’re asking the reader to devote hours of her time to your book. Don't ask her to waste part of her time on meaningless dialog. Make every word count.

"Hi. Seen Joan lately? I can't locate her."

Have I gotten the same idea across, this time with only eight words? Maybe I've gone too far. Maybe it's better to say,

"Hi. Seen Joan lately? I've called and gone by. I can't locate her."

The difference between the eight word version and the thirteen word version comes down to voice. You decide which works best for *your* voice. But don't go for the 66 word version unless you have consciously made a decision to use that bloated version and for a very good reason.

Take a look at your dialog and see if you can draw a line through some of the words and still have the meaning, the essence of what needs to be said, left.

In the movie *The Graduate,* the lawyer gave Benjamin (Dustin Hoffman) one word of advice—"Plastics." I'm going to give you two words to remember when writing dialog – **lean, powerful**.

Exercises

1. Look at the dialog in your latest book, preferably a work in progress. See if you can find pieces of dialog that can be tightened up.

2. Also, look for some dialog where you can use a more powerful statement to get the idea across to the reader, in fewer words.

3. What would you do to improve this section of dialog?

"Mr. Johnson, I'm afraid I'm going to need to take you in to the station for further questioning."

"Wait just a minute. Do you know whom you're dealing with? I'm not just any Mr. Johnson. I'm Jonas Johnson."

"Yes. I know who you are. But that doesn't change the fact that you need to come with me to the local police station."

Chapter 6

Let's Get Un-Real

Okay. Novel dialog. How?

Listen. Listen to dialog everywhere: in the grocery store, a restaurant, the post office, church, political rallies, old men having coffee in a local café, women discussing the latest fashion—or the latest gossip. Listen to what people are saying and how they say it when they are talking to you. Not just the idea they want you to get, but the manner in which they tell you. Keep a notepad and pen handy and jot down notes—not on what they are saying, but how they say it. What made it stand out from other bits of dialog you are listening to?

Wait a minute. Didn't you just tell us that novel dialog was not the same as "real" or "natural" dialog? Yes, I did and I'm sticking with that. Novel dialog is natural dialog *made better*. Listening to conversation around you will give you the cadence, the language, the voice of real dialog. You do not want to copy it down word for word. Remember that novel dialog needs to be *better* than the natural dialog we hear. It is more to the point. It is leaner. It doesn't waste the time of the reader. Most of all, it does not allow the reader's mind to wander, to think of what's for dinner, or to even wonder about the time.

You want to capture the essence of dialog, the cadence, inflection, rhythm, the language, the voice—and then—make it better. Cut out all the unnecessary words. Remember Rule #1 from chapter 5. "Not necessary? Cut it out."

It's like being at the race track, trying to decide how to place your bet. There's advice being spouted all around you. You disregard 99.9% of it until you find the bit of conversation from someone who really knows the horses, the jockeys, the track condition, the weather, and just perhaps any collusion wandering around this particular race. You are very selective. You cut out all the trivial stuff. You keep only what is important.

Same way with dialog. Be selective. Be ruthless. Keep a sharp knife handy (or a finger hovering over the delete key). We could even rephrase Rule #1 to be, "If in doubt, cut it out." If you aren't sure whether it is necessary or desirable, cut it out. Then, go back and reread the section. Does it still make sense? Does it still convey the essence of what you want? Will the reader still understand? If you answer "No" to any of these, then you can execute an "Undo" and put it back. Then, ask yourself two more questions. Have you lost any character enhancement? Did you diminish the movement of the plot? If you answer "Yes" to either of those, put it back in.

I find it rare the discarded words go back in.

Sounds like a lot of trouble.

You've spent six months, maybe nine months, and sometimes years, on this book. You're going to put your name on it. You want it to be the best possible. You want it to sell, not just to a publisher, but to readers.

It is not too much trouble. Dialog is one of the reasons manuscripts are turned down for publication.

So, you listen and develop an ear for how dialog sounds. Inflection. How do people use that to change the meaning?

How do they use that to give their interpretation of "the facts."

Example: "She said it was a brilliant movie."
With the inflection on "she" we realize that the speaker did not agree with that assessment of the movie.

So, when listening to conversation, check the cadence. Is it constant, hesitant, rushed, erratic? And how do they give added value to the words with their hands, face, body? You are not concerned with the content. You are not eavesdropping to find out specific information, although you can learn a lot from that also.

Example: True story. Some months ago, I was in a restaurant with my wife. The people in the next booth were chatting away and I was only vaguely aware of what they were saying. But at one point, my brain zeroed in, realizing somehow, as brains do, that I should hear the words. One of the women said, "Is she the woman who died—twice." I guess my brain was picking up all the conversation, and discarding it as fast as it came in. But, when this scrap of the conversation arrived, my brain made an instant decision that this was worth keeping. Will I use that in a future book? You can count on it.

I've said to pare down the dialog and I've been talking about individual speeches. But, the same should apply to the whole conversation. Try not to have long stretches of dialog. Break it up if at all possible. Please do it in a way that doesn't just go through the motions, but actually enhances the scene. To this end, avoid breaking up the conversation with an unnecessary action. For instance, don't have: a lot of dialog; (Then action) She took a drink. Then more dialog. Unless ... (There is always an "unless" when dealing with writing.) Unless this drink has poison in it, or she has been on the wagon for two years, and this is a martini. Unless, the action adds something other than a break in the quotations marks. Unless the action adds to the plot or enhances a character, just like the dialog does.

Think of how many times you have seen a break in dialog to tell the reader that "she pushed a lock of hair behind her ear." Sometimes, this happens a dozen times in a single book. I'm not the only one who notices this and is pulled out of the book to think, "Why did the writer put that in?" Is it possible that such a movement could be important? Does it tell us the woman is overly concerned with how her hair looks? Possible. But I've never seen it used to help define character.

Keep in mind that what the speaker intends, and does not say, is more important than the actual words. We've all said at one time or another, "That's what he said, but that's not what he meant." You, the writer, would like to write dialog where the reader picks up the real intent. You don't have to spell out every little aspect. Write the dialog so that the reader gets exactly what you want them to get, without going into detail.

Example: "Oh, it was great to be there, to see Jason, ever the gentleman, cut my friend to shreds without ever raising his voice."

We know it was not great to be there. We get the intent: Jason is not a gentleman.

Don't tell your English teacher I said this, but –

Dialog, natural or novel, is not limited to grammatically correct sentences. It isn't limited to sentences. I had an English teacher once who wrote F R A G across any incomplete sentence. I accumulated a few of those. But, today, I'm telling you it is perfectly okay to use fragment sentences, if that matches the speaker. If the speaker is an English teacher, then maybe not, unless this teacher has a different persona outside the classroom.

Some of your characters will not use correct English. As we've mentioned, some will leave out words, sometimes verbs, sometimes the subject of the sentence. If that is appropriate for your character, do it.

Example: "John, will you come here, please."

"Sure. What ya want?"

"I need someone to move this antique table with extreme care. I am unable to move it myself."

"Too heavy for ya?"

"Yes. I'm afraid I might damage it if I try to move it."

"Not me."

Here we have one character using perfect English, and the other character leaving out subject and verb, using incomplete sentences, violating many grammar rules. But it is okay. It happens in dialog and reflects the educational level of the character.

Let me emphasize this point. It is not only okay, but desirable, *if* it helps define the character.

Okay. Listen up.

Write your spare, improved dialog. Then, you must listen to your own dialog. Read it aloud. Listen to how it sounds, as if two (or more) people were actually talking and you were just listening. Often, this will highlight areas that need improving. Often this improvement is a sharp knife (or a quick finger on the delete key). If it doesn't move the plot along or it doesn't enhance our understanding or feeling for a character, slash it out. (I've used "slash" here because I want you to be vicious. Each word must be worth the reader's time.)

Next, have someone else read it. Listen with your eyes closed. Treat it as an audio book. How does that conversation sound? Are you drawn into it, or do you wish they'd get on with the rest of the book?

And an important note. If you change the dialog, then you must read aloud again. Did the change make it better? Can you still improve it? Does it still get across what you want the dialog to accomplish? It certainly occurs that sometimes the "improvement" isn't. If you change the dialog, you must check it, and reading it aloud is the best way.

This is time well spent.

Exercises

1. Write a piece of dialog where some words (maybe subject or verb) in each sentence are left out, without harming the meaning of the dialog.

2. Write a piece of dialog where one person never uses a complete sentence. Make sure when you finish that it reads well and captures the speech of the character.

3. Now, write a short piece of dialog between two characters where their speech is noticeably different. This could be by level of formal education, by ethnicity, by upbringing, whatever. But we should notice a distinctly different dialog from each.

4. Below is a piece of dialog that might be in a novel. Read it through and then determine how you might improve

> it. Write a better version of it. Then, and only then, read the version I propose as an improvement. No fair peeking. Do your own first. Then read mine. Your version will probably be better than mine, but mine might give you some ideas also. Remember, no peeking.

John studied the pieces of the once beautiful statue that his handyman held. "What happened? How did you happen to break it? What were you doing?"

Willie looked down at the fragments in his hands, turned one of them over. "Well, no sir. No, I didn't do nothing to it. When I got here this morning, it was jus' like this then."

John nodded a few times. "You just walked into the library and there the statue was, broken and sitting on the table."

"Well, yeah. I mean, that's what I jus' said."

Here's my attempt to improve it.

John looked at the statue. "You broke it?"
Willie fidgeted a little. "No Sir. Like this when I got here."
"Just lying on the table?"
"Yes, sir."

Chapter 7

Your Honor, My Summation

Summary dialog is text in which you summarize what has been said. In other words, instead of giving the actual dialog, you give the reader a summary of what was said.

Why would you do this? You've learned how to write good, tight, better-than-natural dialog. Why not use that skill and forget the summary bit?

Sometimes the reader already knows the information that will come out in the dialog. You don't want to subject her to plowing through it again. But somebody in the book needs to receive that information from another character. Summarize it.

Example: Gloria hated to be the one to break the news to Hillary, but someone had to do it. So she told her exactly, word for word, what Janice had said, how she said it, and her glee at being able to tell the group what had happened.

Notice, I haven't repeated what Janice said. The reader already knows that. To repeat it here is to waste the reader's time, and patience. Janice's conversation might have run several hundred words. Here, we have summarized it in twenty-eight words. The reader will supply the rest.

Sometimes we use summary dialog even when the reader does not already know the information. It may be that to recreate the situation, the dialog, would be too long, too tedious, slowing the reader at a time that you don't want her to slow down at all. In this case, a character can summarize the dialog, give the gist of the conversation to the reader, give her what she needs, and move on.

Example: Morris slumped down in the booth. "I'm beat."

"Tell me what they said. I want to hear every word, every obscenity."

"No, you don't. They went on for thirty minutes. Wilson stuck to his position on changing the schedule. Mac kept repeating the same argument that keeping to such a rigid schedule only told the burglars when to move in."

"That's it?"

"That's it. Same thing, over and over. I thought I'd scream."

We want the reader to know that Wilson and Mac argued a long time, without changing their positions, but we don't want the reader to have to endure the argument. So, Morris summarizes it for the reader.

What not to do.

Don't give long summaries. I've seen summaries that were as long as the original conversation. Use your delete key and cut long summaries down. This is even more important than avoiding long stretches of dialog. If the reader already knows the information, you only need to say character "A" gave the information to character "B". Period. End of story.

Exercises

1. Write a short section of summary dialog that covers information that the reader already knows.

2. Write a short section of summary dialog that covers information that the reader does not know, but doesn't need all the conversation to understand what was said and get the flavor of how it was said.

Chapters 8 & 9

The Super D

Yeah, it does say chapters 8 and 9. Internalization is the Super D, the Super Dialog, and it is so important, it's worth two chapters. But, I'm going to pack the power of internalization, two chapters' worth, into one chapter. The Super D is worth it.

Confused? Well, let's just get right to it.

Why is Internalization so important? There are three reasons. **Number 1**, internalization will show the true feelings of the character. **Number 2**, internalization will show the true character of the character. (Yes, that is different from number 1.) And **number 3** – the biggie – the readers will believe it.

Let's look at each of those to see why it's important.

First, internal dialog shows the true feelings of the character. When you talk to yourself, you know that no one else can eavesdrop on that conversation. Even with all the advanced technology, no one else knows what you are thinking. Oh, you can give it away with a look, a mannerism, or something else you might do, perhaps unconsciously. But, they cannot actually *know* what you are thinking.

What does that mean? There is no reason to lie or to shade the truth. So, internalization can be expected to give a true picture of the person's thoughts and feelings.

What does this mean to the writer? It is a way to reveal what this character really thinks and feels. Let me illustrate the power of the internalization. (I will put the internal dialog in italics, a common way to indicate internal dialog.)

Example: Two women meet at a class reunion. Natalie says to Janice,

"Hi. Glad to see you here. Someone had said you wouldn't be able to make it this year."

Here we have two friends meeting, apparently glad to see one another. But suppose we have a little internalization from Natalie.

And if I'd known you were coming, I'd have stayed home.

We get two attitudes from Natalie; "Hi, glad to see you." And "I'd have stayed home." Which is the reader going to believe? Without a doubt, the internal thought. Why? Since no one else can hear this, why wouldn't it be the truth?

From personal experience, the reader knows that she herself sometimes says things that are not her real feelings. But she also knows that what she thinks is always the truth.

Example: Rusty finds out that he has received an invitation to attend a special seminar. To a group of his friends he says,

"I've got the time. I guess I'll go. It could be interesting."

But internally, he's thinking,

Wow! This is the greatest. I never thought I'd get accepted. Fantastic.

Now we understand how excited Rusty really is over this invitation. It's not exactly contrary to what he told his friends, but it certainly shows a different emotion. Best of all, the reader will believe the internalized version.

The second reason internalization is such a powerful tool for the writer is that it gives a true picture of the spirit of a character. I'm not talking about his or her thoughts in a particular situation, but the moral fiber of the person. It answers the questions: what makes her tick? What motivates her? What are her real goals? This goes far beyond what she may think at a specific moment. This is not a snapshot of her; it is the global picture of this person.

Example: Ryan leaned against the booth, hoping no one else came to try and pitch a quarter into one of the small dishes. *I hate these charity things. If the poor people would get out, get a job and work like I do, they wouldn't be poor. If I didn't think this might help me get Mildred in the sack, I wouldn't get within a mile of this sham.*

This isn't Ryan's actual thoughts about something he said. This is about Ryan's moral fiber. This is about who Ryan really is, not about a particular conversation. You have given the reader a clear picture of Ryan's personality, at least at this point in his life. And the reader will believe it. Why not? It is after all, Ryan's private thoughts. You, the writer, might be able to salvage Ryan before the book is over. Or not. But at this moment, the reader knows who Ryan really is.

Which leads us to the third and most important and powerful strength of internalization: the reader will believe what comes from internal dialog. After each of the three examples above, I've commented on the fact that the reader will believe it.

Private thoughts can mirror the "true" person because they are private. Do you have some feelings or thoughts that you do not choose to share with anyone, not your mother, not your best friend? Not even your spouse? Of course you do. It could be small, but you'd just as soon keep it to yourself. It could be as simple as thinking, *Will you shut up about your damn dog. That's all you talk about*. But you don't say it because, while you would like to hear less about the dog, this is your friend and you do not want to hurt her feelings.

In a book, you can let the reader hear those "private" revelations. In real life, we don't have access to these thoughts of another person. However, you, the writer, can give the reader this important information. And the reader will believe it.

It is why fiction can sometimes be more powerful than non-fiction. In fiction, you, the writer, can give the reader insight into the character's mind, his most private thoughts and feelings. Non-fiction, because it is supposed to be a true depiction of what we actually know, cannot do that.

Don Quixote and the windmills.

In the book Don Quixote, a Spanish novel by Miguel de Cervantes, the protagonist sets out to revive chivalry, loses touch with reality and begins to see windmills as giants that he has to fight.

Those of you who have read my book on character development (*Character: The Heartbeat of the Novel*) know that Cyrano de Bergerac is one of my favorite characters. In the play, Cyrano's arch enemy Count de Guiche says,

"Do you know Don Quixote?"

Cyrano says, "Yes, and find myself the hero."

De Guiche says, "Remember, the long arms may sweep round and cast you down into the mire."

And Cyrano replies, "Or up ... into the sky."

That is a long way to say that internalization is very powerful. It can raise the level of your novel, or it can cause you trouble.

So let me give you three caveats.

First, internalization can only come from the POV (Point Of View) character. It is only that character whose mind you, the writer, can open up to the reader. If the POV character changes in the next chapter, then you can give access *only* to the new POV character's internal thoughts.

The second point is that because internalization is so powerful, it can be overdone. You do not want the reader to be privy to every thought your character has. Pick and choose. A few well chosen bits of internalization can reveal a lot about the person. Too much gets tiresome.

There's another reason to use internalization judiciously. As with many powerful things, if used too much, too often, it begins to lose power. You could think of it as similar to a speaker with a full, booming voice. And then, at some point his voice drops to a soft level. Now, everybody is straining to hear what has caused this change. If he spoke softly all the time, it would have little power. Who would notice it?

The same thing is true with internalization. If we hear all of a character's thoughts, or even a lot of them, it becomes, "Ho Hum. Another thought."

So, use internalization for places where you want to really get the reader's attention, where you want to make a strong point, where you want to "set the record straight." This is the truth, the true person; pay attention.

Third, be careful about having access to the thoughts of too many characters. This can be confusing to the reader. Often, just the thoughts of the protagonist, and possibly the antagonist, are sufficient. And always, internal thoughts come only from the POV character. As a rule (if there were any rules here), keep internalizations short.

Use internalization carefully, judiciously. Pick the places where it will do the most good, have the greatest impact. But, DO USE IT. It is one of the strongest tools in the writer's toolbox.

Exercises

1. Write a bit of dialog followed by a piece of internal dialog which shows the person's real feeling, which is contrary to what he had just said. It could be contrary in either direction: more positive or more negative.

2. Write a piece of internal dialog which tells the reader something significant about the true moral compass of a character. Again, this can be a positive thing, or a negative thing.

3. Write a brief segment of internal dialog that gives the reader a very different picture of a character than the reader gets from looking at the public persona of the character.

4. Write a piece of internal dialog from the protagonist which tells the reader how the character really feels about the goal he needs to achieve in this book.

5. Write a piece of internal dialog which tells the reader whether the protagonist thinks he can achieve this goal or not.

6. Write a piece of internal dialog from the antagonist where he shares why he must defeat the protagonist.

Chapter 10

Fight, Fight

Dialog is an excellent place to set up conflict between characters. Someone in the back of the room is asking if conflict isn't plot and not part of dialog.

Most certainly, conflict is the soul of plot. No conflict, no interest. Whether romance, comic capers, thrillers, sci fi, fantasy, or humor, conflict will play a big part in developing the plot.

Remember the good advice you often get: "Add more conflict. Try to get it on every page." That's where dialog can help out.

Conflict between two people

You can add little bits of conflict here and there – on every page – by use of dialog. And not just minor conflict. The level is up to you. Here's a little example we gave in chapter 4.

Example: "You sound different today."
"No I don't."

Now, you might say, that's not much conflict. That's okay. Every instance of conflict does not have to be an all out war.

But, actually, even this seven word conflict can be as much as you want. It can be slight. "No, I'm fine." Or you can make it much stronger when the second person is hiding something. Whom that affects, and how it affects him or her, can determine the degree of conflict.

Suppose the first person, a woman, has never met the second person, a man. She has only talked to him on the telephone. Now he sounds different. Is it the same man? Depending on the place, time and circumstances, you could develop this into a good scene.

Or perhaps the second person has been threatened by a vicious person who made it clear her child would be killed if she let anyone know about his threat. She is still terrified and her voice is not the same. If the first person pushes it, this can become a full-fledged conflict. But we've set it up in just seven words of dialog.

Powerful stuff, this dialog.

Think about your novel. How many instances of small conflicts can you add through dialog? Of course, you need to make certain that the conflict fits in nicely with the story. Don't force it. Look at your characters and determine which ones will be willing to disagree at the drop of a hat. You may have a character who is going through a bad time and is generally mad at the world. He may take exception to almost everything that is said to him.

Example: My comments are within parenthesis.

"That was a great movie."

"No it wasn't. It was terrible. I can't believe you liked it."

(A little conflict. Want some more?)

"Oh, I'm sorry you didn't like it. I didn't mean to push my opinion off on you."

"Stop it. Don't be so wishy-washy on everything. You liked it. I didn't. That's it."

(Okay, just a little more.)

"Sorry."

"Don't say you're sorry. There nothing to be sorry about. We disagree."

(And of course it could go on. But enough for us right now.)

They will still remain friends, but we've added conflict through dialog. And by the way, we've enhanced the reader's understanding of both characters.

I Want; They Want

Sometimes it isn't a conflict, just different agendas. Each participant in a dialog may have a different parti pris. Have you made the bias clear to the reader? Or perhaps you hold that back for introduction later. So there may be no real conflict, but different backgrounds, different goals, or just different information.

Perhaps this will come out in the conversation. One person could convince the other on some point. Or not. Again, this can be a simple disagreement, or a real conflict. Decide before you start this dialog what you want to come out of it.

Of course, it is possible that the purpose of this particular dialog is to have one person convince another person to change their position on some item. You decide whether that change takes place or not—before you start the dialog.

It's me against me!

(I guess grammatically it should be, "It's I against me." But, even though correct, it will stop the average reader. Your book has to read smoothly and sometimes, by a conscious choice, you need to violate a grammar rule.)

The conflict can be within one character. In fact, this is often the case. Certainly Hamlet had a pretty good conflict going on inside his own mind. This will most often be expressed for the reader with internal dialog.

Example: He looked through the wallet he had picked up off the sidewalk. There were credit cards, driver's license, other cards. And a wad of money. *I could keep the money, sort of a finder's fee. Return the rest. Say I found the wallet but there was no money in it. Who would know?* He looked at the stack of hundred dollar bills. *I would know.*

Here, conflict exists, not with another person, but within himself. And this conflict will further the plot, and allow the reader to know this character better.

Example: *I could ask her. But she hardly knows me. I've never spoken to her before. Still, there's no bus in sight and it's starting to rain.*

Here, we have a situation that is not a matter of life or death. Maybe. So, it could be a very minor conflict: offer her a ride or not. Of course, we don't know what's going to happen next. Maybe it *is* a matter of life and death; the reader just doesn't know it.

I'm Surrounded by Problems!

Some minor things can create stress. One person in the conversation is impatient—not willing to explain or wait. A little tension can quickly appear.

Or a simple misunderstanding can introduce tension. By the way, this can be a real misunderstanding, or one that is artificially introduced. And if it's artificial, why did that character cause it?

What if one person answers a question by asking his own question? Depending on how it's done, it can be simple, or quite annoying.

What if one participant responds with a smart-alecky comment?

By now, I think you are seeing that getting a little conflict on every page is duck soup using dialog.

Reality against public image

We all have a public persona and it does not always agree with who we really are. When you have a character where this is the case, internal dialog is the perfect vehicle to expose this.

Example: John has a public persona, a façade, of being a nice guy, gentle and caring. But in fact, that is not the "true" John. In this scene, Annie, a girl he is interested in, has brought her little Chihuahua with her. John tells her what a cute dog it is and pets it. But we get this bit of internalization.

Given the opportunity, I'd kill that little rat. Twist its ugly head right off its body. I hate little dogs. I'd like to pile all the little varmints in a pit, pour gasoline over them and light it. Watch them fry. Now, those would be hot dogs I could really like.

Now we get a very different picture of John. Which will the reader believe? What the man thinks can usually be depended on to give the true picture. Why not? No one else is privy to his thoughts. He can afford to "tell it like he is."

Now I agree, that is a pretty extreme example I just gave. I did that on purpose to make the change from public image to actual character inordinate. You don't have to be as extravagant. You may just want to point out that he is not as nice as Annie thinks.

So, internal dialog is another opportunity to inject some conflict into the book, always a good idea. Internalization is a very powerful tool. Use it carefully, wisely. Don't overuse it. Don't pound the reader over the head with it.

But do use it.

Exercises

1. Write a very brief (two lines) bit of regular dialog which establishes a minor conflict.

2. Write a very brief (two lines) bit of regular dialog that hints (foreshadows) a major conflict.

3. Write a brief segment of internalization which shows a conflict with another character.

4. Write a brief segment of internalization which shows a conflict within the character thinking.

5. Write a brief segment of internalization which shows the reader something he hasn't known before.

6. Write a brief segment of internalization which changes, or adds to, the picture the reader had of a particular character.

7. Write a brief bit of internalization which gives the reader a clue not known before.

8. Write a brief bit of internalization which provides a little foreshadowing.

9. Write a little dialog in which one character answers a question with a question. Did the character need clarification, or was she trying to change the direction of the dialog?

10. Write a little dialog where one participant pretends to misunderstand what another person said. How does the other person react? Where does this discussion go?

Chapter 11

Who Said That?

Attribution is an aspect of dialog where many people have problems. Some of the problems are the result of poor advice from other writers. So, let's talk about what needs to be done, what to avoid, and where the simplest approach is often the best.

The two most important points on attribution are these. First, you seldom want the reader to have even a moment's doubt as to who is speaking. In mysteries or thrillers there can be instances where you *do* want some doubt. That is the exception. The rule is, never make the reader wonder, even for a second, who is speaking. The second point is, you do not want to give needless information or slow down the reader with unnecessary or convoluted attribution.

If you have just two people in the conversation, and you've identified who is speaking at the onset, then little attribution is necessary thereafter. Even here, if you have a long conversation, you need to identify a speaker occasionally. You never want the reader to stop and go back, tracing through to see who made a particular statement. Not only have you stopped the reader, never a good thing, but you have probably irritated her as well.

Another situation to consider is a break in the conversation. This may be some interruption or some action. Now you must make certain that the reader knows who is speaking when the conversation resumes.

Example: Sam and Ed are talking.

"I haven't seen him in over a year," Sam said.
"I haven't either."
"I wonder what happened."
A loud noise from outside caused both men to put their glasses down, walk over and look out the window. A young kid was walking by, his boom box held on his shoulder. The men just shook their heads.
"I used to see him all the time."

Who said "I used to see him all the time"? It isn't clear. And while it may or may not be important who said that particular line, now the reader doesn't know the sequence of the conversation. And somewhere in the next few lines it might be important to know who is speaking. So, if there is a break in the conversation, tell the reader who picks up the conversation after the break.

The problem here is, you, the author, know who is speaking. There is never any doubt in your mind. You are the one who decides who is speaking. This means you often don't recognize there is a problem. Look for it.

Two's company, three's a crowd

However, once you have three or more people in the conversation, attribution becomes more important. Now, the reader needs to know who is speaking. One has finished, but there are multiple persons to pick from for the next speech. So we need to tell the reader who said it.

The simplest and most effective way to do this is simply say, "John said," "Mary said," "Bill said." I know that many people do not like said. And they certainly do not like to use it often. But the reality is, "he said" is almost invisible to the reader. The mind notes the "who" but passes right over the "said." So, do not be afraid to use the simple "said."

Elmore Leonard is generally recognized as a master at dialog. Stephen King has certainly gathered in the fans. Both advocate using "said." Leonard, in his ten rules of writing, says to stick with said. He thinks you should never use other verbs in place of said. King echoes that same sentiment. Larry McMurtry's books rarely use anything else. Stick with "said."

If you have a long sequence where you need an attribute on almost every line, and the segments of speech are short, then it might be appropriate to vary the verb so that there is not a long list of, "John said," "Jim said," "Bill said," over and over. Use judgment. To say never use anything else but "said," makes as little sense as to say you must never use "said." On that point, I can disagree with Leonard. But I suspect he was making a point that you should shy away from all the substitute verbs.

When appropriate, you can certainly use other descriptors for said, such as whined, mumbled, whispered, yelled and other such verbs. But, be certain that it applies. And do not overuse those. Stick those in too much and the reader gets tired of it. You should make the *dialog* show us that the person was whining, or mumbling, or muttering, or yelling. You are much better off to make the dialog speak.

A NO, NO.

Please avoid implying the impossible. A person cannot smile a word. (I'm certain that many a young girl can smile an invitation, but that is really an *implied* invitation. She did not smile the words.)

Bad Example: "That was an excellent chapter," she smiled.

She cannot smile words.

Correct Example: "That was an excellent chapter." She smiled.

The period and closed quotation mark after "chapter" signals that she has stopped speaking. She certainly can smile while she's speaking or after she finishes speaking.

Bad Example: She sneezed, "I have to hurry."

Again, she can't sneeze out words.

Correct Example: She sneezed. "I have to hurry."

The period after "sneezed" separates it from the actual words. She can certainly sneeze just before she speaks.

Another Example: "I am going—." She sneezed. "to the doctor."

We're okay here. Clearly, the sneeze interrupted her statement.

Where's the Action?

Akin to this is the use of action for attribution. This is a very acceptable way of giving attribution without putting in "said" or any verbs to take the place of said. However, the action should be natural, should fit in properly, and should fit the person and situation. You do not want to simply throw in some action to avoid using "said." Here is an example in which action/attribution is used properly.

Example: Martin reached for his gun. "It's time for both of you to leave."

In this case, the action is natural, important even, and it tells us who is speaking.

Example: "Let's go." Roger grabbed his briefcase. "We're going to be late."

Let's say there are three people in the office. We need attribution. This is a natural action that fits in properly and tells us who is speaking.

On the other hand, here is the type of action/attribution that you want to avoid.

Bad Example: June scratched her nose. "I've only one final left to take."

Unless there is some significance to June scratching her nose, don't use the action. The reader will know you are forcing it. If, however, June is going to start her nose bleeding and not be able to make her final exam, then it would be appropriate to use this action/attribution. Otherwise, take it out or replace it with a proper attribution if one is needed.

Try to avoid getting into a rut. Find some other action besides "raising her eyebrows," or "picked up his cup." Those might be okay once a book. But I've read novels in which some of the characters had very active eyebrows, chapter after chapter. Then, it is the *reader* who is raising her eyebrows. (This is one I have to work to avoid.)

One last comment on action. If some *significant* action is necessary, don't relegate it to attribution. If it's important, let the action have its own space.

The Name's the Game

Sometimes it is permissible to use names within the conversation to identify the person being spoken to. If there are only two people in the conversation, then this also identifies the speaker. This should be used carefully. By that, I mean, use it only when it makes sense in the scene. But, as a rule, people do not address others by name in the course of conversation. Here is an example where using names is not appropriate.

Example: "Jim, I don't think Bob is coming."
"I guess you're right, Ron."

It's not likely that Ron and Jim would call the other by name in this case. This is an example of how it should not be used.

But, sometimes, it is suitable.

Example: "Now you listen to me, Jim Barton. I will oppose you every step of the way."

The name fills the job of attribution (by telling who is being addressed, if not who is actually speaking), but its main function is to emphasize the seriousness of the statement. It is natural here.

The Dreaded Adverb

There are many professional writers who would ban adverbs from all literature. It was Will Rogers who said, "If you see an adverb, kill it." There are certainly places where an adverb can earn its keep. But those places should be few and far between in dialog.

This was not always the case. In the early twentieth century, Victor Appleton (pseudonym originally for Edward Stratemeyer and then others, principally Howard Garis) turned out many books whose protagonist was Tom Swift, a young inventor who also solved mysteries and defeated many people who tried to steal his inventions. Swift never "said" anything without some adverb to modify the "said." The use was so consistent that eventually the practice was dubbed "a Swifty." There are even party games to make Swifty puns, such as the following.

"That's because I'm a proctologist," he said cheekily.

Or ...

"Oh my. We'd better call the plumber," she said with a flush.

Or ...

"I guess we should go to the cemetery," he said gravely.

So, unless you want to be called A Swifty, avoid using adverbs to modify "said" or words that substitute for "said."

Selecting better verbs or stronger verbs can usually make the use of an adverb modifier unnecessary.

Example: "Don't tell John we're here," she said softly.
"Don't tell John we're here," she whispered.

Example: "I won't go," she said emphatically.
"I will not, under any circumstance, go," she said.
Or, "Understand this. I will not go," she said.

In the first example, we used "whispered" which takes care of both "said" and "softly." In the second example, we have changed the actual dialog to make the use of "emphatically" totally unnecessary. (Please note, in the preceding sentence, I could leave out the adverb "totally" and still have the meaning I want. So, cut out the adverb.)

R U E

You've probably seen RUE scribbled on your draft by people critiquing your work. This applies to dialog as well as narrative. **R**esist the **U**rge to **E**xplain. This happens when you add words or phrases that simply *tell* the reader what you've already shown (or told) the reader.

Example: "I'm sorry," she said apologetically.

You've already said "sorry." The reader knows what that means. Don't insult the reader by explaining, as if she didn't know what "sorry" meant.

Often, the use of an adverb after dialog is an example of explaining what the reader already knows. RUE.

Example: "No. I won't go. Don't even mention it. No." She was adamant.

After reading the dialog, the reader knows she was adamant. Don't tell the reader. RUE.

Test. If you need to explain, maybe you didn't say it well enough. When you have the urge to explain, try to rephrase and eliminate the urge to explain.

Don't Lose Your Voice

Another way to eliminate many attributions is to have a distinct voice for your characters. While this is not always possible—to the extent that the reader always knows who is speaking—it is a goal.

Example: Dusty pushed through the saloon doors and watched as a stranger, dressed in Eastern clothes, nearly fell off his horse, then hurried up the steps. He stopped in front of Dusty and took several deep breathes.

"Looks like you been caught in the middle of a stampede."

"My wife. We got separated on the road to Gun Barrel. I can't find her."

"Was she saddled up?"

"Saddled up? Oh, yes. She was on a smallish, brown horse."

"You just belly up to the bar and settle them nerves. I'll find her."

"Do you believe you can return her safely? I am most concerned."

"Aw, yeah. I aim to bring that gal back safe as Mother's milk."

"I sincerely hope so. I hardly know where to turn. She is very important to me."

"Well, you just set a spell. Quicker'n a frog's tongue I'll bring that gal back to ya."

No need for attribution here. We know when Dusty's speaking and we know when Walton Richards is talking.

It isn't always possible to differentiate with the actual dialog. But it should be a goal to make the speech patterns, language, and pace distinct for each character. We'll discuss what I call the dialog signature of a character in the next chapter.

Let me wind up this chapter with emotional dialog. In a heated discussion, a bitter argument, or a fight it's the words that count. Make the words convey the scene. Let the dialog be the action. And maybe you will need very little attribution.

So, what should you take away from this chapter? I'd like to say, "All of it." But, the key points are these.

Don't be afraid of "said," but use some judgment.

Select better verbs and better dialog.

Avoid Swifties (adverbs).

Use action for attribution only when it fits.

Strive for a distinct voice for each of your characters so attribution is less important.

Exercises

1. Write a bit of dialog and use an action to handle the attribution. Be sure the action is appropriate for the time, place, character, and dialog.

2. Write a Swifty pun. Then, rewrite the dialog with the adverb absolutely not needed. (Couldn't I have left out the word "absolutely" and gotten the exact same meaning?)

3. Write a bit of dialog between two characters where no attribution is necessary because of the distinct voice of each.

4. Take the piece of dialog from exercise 3 and add a third person into the dialog. How do you handle the attribution so the reader always knows who is speaking?

5. Write (or at least repeat) this sentence: It is okay to use "said" in attribution.

6. Write a bit of dialog between two people that is interrupted so that you need an attribution for the person speaking after the interruption.

7. Write a piece of dialog where it is appropriate for the characters to address one another by name.

8. Write a piece of dialog, not too long but requires two paragraphs, to show us how the quotation marks should be used.

9. Write a piece of dialog from one person that is interrupted by a cough.

10. Here is a piece of dialog.

    Ethan looked at the group anxiously waiting for him to immediately give them clear directions.

    "Guys, I don't have the answers," he said nervously.

    "Ah, what do you mean?" Roger asked cautiously.

    "Come on, Ethan." Jonathan stood quickly. "We depend on you to easily sort things out."

    Ethan slowly shook his head. "This is—"

Sam promptly interrupted him. “Why don’t we quietly leave and give you time to figure this out.”

Rewrite the passage above without adverbs, but stronger verbs. Some of it might require a little more than leaving out the adverb. Improve it.

Chapter 12

The Character's Signature

I'm sure you have all looked at the Declaration of Independence, or at least a copy of it. When you look at the bottom, one name stands out: John Hancock of Massachusetts.

Lewis Morris of New York signed with a bit of a flourish, but it is generally unnoticed. And the signature of Th. Jefferson of Virginia is hardly noticed at all. You have to search for it. But today, over 200 years later, we say, "Put your John Hancock on the dotted line."

Signatures count. And John's stood out. He wanted the English to recognize his signature, to recognize him, to remember him. We certainly remember him.

Okay, so what? We're talking about writing books and specifically writing dialog. What's that have to do with signatures?

Ideally, each of your major characters will have a signature. In this case, I'm talking about a dialog signature. What does your character sound like? What is distinctive about his or her voice? Do you know? Have you thought about it?

When you make up a bio, or character sketch, for major characters, consider including the character's dialog signature.

Whoa. That sounds interesting, but what does it mean? It means write down significant and unique (among your characters) aspects about the character's speech, such as:

Cadence
Vocabulary (word choice)
Diction
Inflection
Accent
Regional dialect
Sentence structure (or lack of)
Flow
Volume
Eye contact
Mannerisms
Ease
Body language
Favorite words
Marker words

Most of those are obvious, but let me comment on a few. Eye contact, mannerisms, body language will not be exhibited in the actual words the character says, but in her actions associated with her dialog. These can be while she's talking, or immediately preceding or following her talking.

Example: Jean pursed her lips and closed her eyes for a moment before speaking. "As I guess you know by now, ..."

Example: Throughout the lengthy answer, not once did Arthur look at me.

Example: Wilma's answer came rather smoothly, but she shredded the tissue she held.

Studies have shown that as much as 50% of information is passed through non-verbal means. And sometimes all the important information is passed visually. So, eye contact, mannerisms, ease, and body language can be considered part of the dialog. Those can pass information, can communicate, and in certain cases, do so more effectively than words.

Don't fail to pay attention to those non-verbal parts of dialog.

Keep in mind, that to be part of the character's signature dialog, these must happen often, not just in a single instance. That is, Jean must generally stop and think before answering. Arthur must avoid eye contact as a rule, and Wilma must be a nervous Nellie when talking to others.

If, in fact, Wilma is normally not nervous but in this instance she is, there must be a reason. What has caused her to be so nervous just now? Or if Arthur normally looks a person straight in the eye, what has caused him to avoid that contact now? If you established the dialog signature so the reader (unconsciously) knows what to expect, when you change that pattern the reader will know something unusual has happened, or is about to happen.

What do I mean by marker words? Those are superfluous words or phrases that add nothing. Some examples are: really, pretty much, little, basically, currently, well, ah, you know. These are what I call empty calorie words. They add no meaning, just fat.

Example: "Well, you know, I basically have pretty much told you all I really know."

What the person really said was, "I've told you all I know." In my example, I've thrown in a bunch of marker words. Usually, a character will have *one or two marker words* that he or she uses frequently. Here's an example of two characters speaking. Can you pick out the marker word for each?

Example: "You really ought to go."
"Well, I just don't know," said Robert.
"It's really important."
"It's just the time. I've got things to do."
"I know. And I really do understand. Still, it's only one day."
"Well, give me some time to think about it. I can't just decide without asking Mary."

As with empty calorie foods, we can use the empty meaning marker words. Just don't overdo it. We don't want too much fat in our dialog.

And did you get both marker words for Robert?

Here are two examples of dialog signature. The same information is delivered, but which version I use depends on the dialog signature I have chosen for Janice.

Example: The policewoman took a seat across the table from Janice. "Tell me what you saw at the shooting."

"Not much."

"Can you tell me what you *did* see?"

"It appeared the big man had knocked the smaller man down."

"And what happened next."

"The smaller man pulled a pistol out of his pocket and shot the bigger man."

"Anything else?"

"I dialed 9-1-1."

Now, here is the same interview, but I've given Janice a different dialog signature.

Example: The policewoman took a seat across the table from Janice. "Tell me what you saw at the shooting."

"Well, I had just turned the corner when I saw the two men, so I didn't see what got it started."

"Can you tell me what you did see?"

"Well, I didn't actually see it, but it looked to me like they must have had an argument and the bigger man knocked the smaller man down. The small guy was on the ground and this big guy was standing over him."

"And what happened next."

"The guy on the ground, the little one, reached in his pocket and pulled out something. Well, at first I didn't know what it was, but then, he turned it and aimed it at the guy standing up. Then, I saw it was a pistol. I don't know what kind it was. I don't know much about guns. But it wasn't a big gun. Just a small hand gun. Like I said, he aimed it at the guy standing over him and he, well, he just pulled the trigger. Just shot the guy."

"Anything else?"

"Well, I didn't know what to do and for a minute I just stood there and watched the big guy fall down. He almost fell on the little man, but he – the little guy – rolled out of the way. Finally, I realized I needed to do something. So, I pulled my cell phone out of my purse and dialed 9-1-1 and told the woman who answered that there was a shooting on 12th street."

Even before I start the book, I know how a character will react in such a situation. I have decided on her dialog signature. It will stay with her throughout the novel.

It may be she stretches out the information, or she uses as few words as possible, short choppy sentences or fragments. It may be that she has a regional dialect. It may be that she has a habit of emphasizing every verb. Perhaps she can't utter a verb without following with an adverb. Maybe she has perfect diction and a powerful vocabulary. What if she talks too loud, or almost whispers regardless of whom she's talking to or where they are? You can give the character one or two marker words that show up in almost every conversation, though they add nothing to what she is saying.

Here's an example of a dialog signature that I might write for a character in one of my books.

Example:

Michael – Dialog Signature

Flow: Very deliberate person – thinks before responding

Mannerism: Frequently begins with "Mmmm." This may be because he is considering an appropriate response.

Cadence or Speech pattern – slow; not rushed

Sentence structure: Complete sentences

Vocabulary – normal with occasional words outside normal, but not esoteric. Examples: paradigm, caveat

Diction – excellent

Regional dialect or **accent**: none

Body language: If asked a question which requires a thoughtful answer, he may nod several times before answering.

Ease and **Volume**: easy, soft spoken

Eye contact: Always makes good eye contact.

Marker word: "Precisely" Marker phrase: "In my opinion."

If I keep this in mind, I will have an easy time writing dialog for Michael.

If the writer sticks carefully with a dialog signature, the reader will (subconsciously) pick up a lot about the speaker. Let's suppose Dan Johnson needs to do a particular task, one he is a little uncertain about how to start. Here are three examples of how different characters might speak to him, if they were there.

> **Example**: Person number 1: "Well now, brother, I reckon you can just about figure that out for yourself."
>
> **Example**: Person number 2: "You're not an idiot. Figure it out."
>
> **Example**: Person number 3: "I would suggest, Mr. Johnson, that you study the situation and come up with an appropriate approach."

The statements tell you a good bit about the person addressing Dan. Or suppose Dan's wife is the one who speaks to him. Here are four different examples of what she might say, depending on how I crafted her dialog signature.

> **Example**: Wife statement 1: "I could tell you, Dan. But I'd rather you decide for yourself."
>
> **Example**: Wife statement 2: "Dear, you know you've done this before. You can do it again."
>
> **Example**: Wife statement 3: "Don't make me have to tell you every step to take. Use your head, Dan."
>
> **Example**: Wife statement 4: "I didn't take you to raise. You're a grown man. Just work it out."

Each one tells the reader about the character of the wife, and also about the relationship between Dan and his wife.

Just as each of us has a different written signature, your characters should have distinct dialog signatures. And for each character, it is best to decide on the signature *before* you introduce the character to your readers. If you've done this, when you get to this scene between Dan and his wife, you already know how she will address the situation.

The key point is, you decide what dialog signature you want for the character. Write it down. (You don't have to include every item I mentioned when I listed what can go into a dialog signature.) Utilize this signature throughout the book. It will help the reader identify the speaker, come to know the character, and not need as much attribution for this character. It will help you the writer maintain a consistent depiction of the character.

Exercises

1. Write a dialog signature for one of the characters from your work-in-progress. Now, write a bit of dialog that conforms to this signature.
2. Write a different dialog signature for another member of your cast. Write the same dialog content you used in the first exercise, but following this new dialog signature.
3. Write a little section of dialog where non-verbal aspects convey much of the message. Or maybe it conveys *all* the *important* parts.
4. Write a short piece of dialog where a character follows his or her dialog signature perfectly.

5. Take the same piece of dialog from exercise 4, but now some unusual circumstance causes the character to abandon some part of dialog signature. As a side note, explain what the circumstance was and how it affected the character.

Chapter 13

Different Folks, Different Jokes

While we like to talk about consistency in dialog—and in all sorts of things—in fact, there are times when the dialog of a character needs to change. That is to say, the speaker will naturally tailor his dialog to his audience.

Actors, stand up comics, and certainly politicians, all adjust their delivery depending on the audience they are addressing. Concerts are tailored to the anticipated audience. All of these performers understand that different groups of people want and expect different things.

You, the writer, must apply that same understanding to your characters. You need to let the character adjust his dialog to the audience he is addressing, unless you have a particularly dense character, or perhaps one who has disdain for everybody he talks to. This adjustment means that depending on who he is talking to, he may use a different vocabulary, or a different tone, or a different pace, or a different diction, maybe even a different set of grammar rules (or lack of any grammar at all).

Example: Johnny has had a little altercation with his nemesis Bobby. Johnny has been called to the Principal's office.

"Well, ah, Mr. Wilson, it was just a mistake. Bobby wanted one of my cupcakes. He all the time wants my desserts. So I, ah, you know, tossed it to him. But I guess he sort of just turned away at that moment. I think somebody yelled at him. And it just sort of hit him in the back."

Later, Johnny's walking home with some of his friends.

"You should a seen him. Got 'em right in the butt. Looked like he messed his pants. Big bad Bobby boy crapped his pants. Everybody's laughing at him."

At home, Johnny's mother asks him about the incident at school.

"What? Old Wilson called you? Wasn't nothing to it, Mom. Bobby's always bugging me to give him part of my lunch. So I gave him some."

Here, we have the same person telling about the same incident, but to different audiences. Three different audiences, three different descriptions, different words, different sentence structures.

Remember who the audience is. Tailor the dialog not only to the person speaking, but also to the audience.

Let's look at another example.

Example: Mr. Johnson is the CEO of his company. He's talking to his Board of Directors.

"Gentlemen, I've placed before you a comprehensive plan for our next five years. You will want to review it with diligence. At our next board meeting we will discuss the salient points. Then, if no major pitfalls are discovered, we'll ratify it and present it to our stockholders. This outlines our goals. My challenge to you is to exceed these, to propel this company, our company, to the pinnacle of our sector."

Mr. Johnson is also the grandfather of two young girls. He visits with them that same evening.

“How’re my girls doing? I know you wouldn’t expect anything from ol’ granddad, but I brought you something anyway. How ‘bout a funny, funny book. And if you give me a hug, I might even read it to you. How’s that sound?”

Here, we have the same character, but different audiences and different subject matter. He wouldn’t talk to the Board of Directors like he talks to his granddaughters. Likewise, he would not talk to his granddaughters in the same way he addresses the Board of Directors.

If he had a secret life and dealt with drug dealers, he would have a different manner of speech and a different dialog when talking to them. Different audiences, different voices, different vocabulary, different manner. If he addressed the drug dealers as he does the Board of Directors, he would probably get his throat cut. If he addressed his grandchildren like he talked to the drug dealers, he would lose them. And so on.

Your readers know whom the character is talking to. And they know that it is important for him to keep his audience in mind and adjust his dialog to match. You, the writer, must do the same thing.

Exercises

1. Select a character who is likely to talk to two different categories of people, two different audiences. Let him tell each the same basic information. But have him adjust his speech, his diction, his grammar, his tone, and his vocabulary to match each of the audiences.

2. In my example above with Mr. Johnson, suppose the CEO lets some “board of directors” words slip into his conversation with his grandchildren. Is that

reasonable? Would it be more realistic if he did let a couple of those words slip in? If he did, would the children ask about the words? Would the granddad catch himself and reword? Or maybe define the words? How would you handle that? Write a little piece with the CEO talking to his grandchildren and a word or two slip in that are far above the children's learning.

Chapter 14

Howdy Pardna

Dialect can be thought of as a characteristic of speech associated with a particular group of people. This could be characteristics typical of a particular region, a particular social class, or a particular ethnic group. It can also be a result of the consistent but improper use of the language by a group of people.

It could be simply the change in a language. All languages change over time. And languages vary according to place and social setting.

A dialect is distinguished by its vocabulary, grammar, and pronunciation. This is different from an accent, which is the emphasis by pitch and/or stress, given to a particular syllable or word in speaking. However, for our purposes, much of what applies to dialect also applies to the use of an accent for a character. I will use dialect to include both.

In the play Pygmalion, the protagonist Henry Higgins claimed to be able to tell where a person came from in England within a few miles just by listening to the person speak. England, with 1,500 years of spoken language has many dialects in the various regions of the country. Even today, it is often possible to tell where an English person comes from to within about 15 miles or less, so I'm told.

But for the writer, dialect is a mixed blessing. It must be done with extreme care, otherwise the reader will quickly tire of it. Either you've put the reader in a bad mood, or you've lost her altogether. On the other hand, dialect may be desirable to create the setting, the feeling of the place and time.

There is certainly enough precedence for using dialect. D.H. Lawrence used dialect, but with restraint. Harper Lee used dialect to capture the feel of a small Alabama town during the depression. The popular middle grade book *Dovey Coe* was replete with dialect. Here is a passage from the book.

Example: "My name is Dovey Coe and I reckon it don't matter if you like me or not. I'm here to lay the record straight, to let you know them folks saying I done a terrible thing are liars. I aim to prove it, too. I hated Parnell Caraway as much as the next person, but I didn't kill him."

Note that we get the flavor without the aftertaste. The reader does not have to slow down or stop to decide how something is pronounced or what the meaning of a word is.

That is the key to using dialect well. Often is takes only a few words to let the reader know where this character comes from and perhaps his background. "Y'all just mozy on along," gives us a lot of background on the speaker. He certainly isn't from New York, Boston, or any place up east.

Here are a couple of examples from *To Kill a Mockingbird.*

Example: Walter Cunningham says, "Almost died first year I come to school and et them pecans—folks say he pizened 'em and put 'em over on the school side of the fence."

Example: Calpurnia's son Zeebo says to Scout's older brother, "Mister Jem, we're mighty glad to have y'all here.

Don't pay no 'tention to Lula, she's contentious because Reverend Sykes threatened to church her."

And Scout comments that Calpurnia uses language differently at church than she does in their home. Scout said Calpurnia has command of two languages.

This is an example of tailoring your language to the audience, as we discussed in chapter 13. Isn't that something we all do? One language for church or the court house, another for the family and perhaps a third for friends.

This should apply to the characters in your book as well.

Here's one last example of the use of dialect by a master, Mark Twain, from Tom Sawyer.

Example: "Ain't he played me tricks enough for me t'know better? But old fools is the biggest fools there is. He 'pears t'know just how long he can tease a body before the anger starts."

It reads easily. There's nothing to slow the reader, but Twain accomplishes what he intends to accomplish.

In reality, it is difficult to write dialect that reads smoothly. It takes practice. And it requires you to read and reread your passages, read them out loud, and then ask someone else to read the passage out loud while you listen.

Sometimes, you can find a few words that will be recognized as unique to a group of people. "Y'all" puts us in the south. "You know" puts us in the younger generation. "I have no idear where he's gone," tells us he's from Boston. "Dis" and "bling" are associated with the black community, although both are creeping into more general use. "He's a burro," meaning "He's an idiot," would put the person in the Mexican group. If you can use some words that point to a specific group, that may be all you need to set the stage.

When a heavier dialect is required, it is best to give a little of it when the character is first introduced, and then slack off.

Example: "Put dis in yo mouf'n chaw it."

Example: "Leuk ower the winno."

This type of dialect requires phonetic spelling. This is one of the most difficult things to put into dialog and have it read smoothly. Or to allow the reader to read it in the natural flow of things and not get tied up with it. How many times have you run across phonetic spelling in a book and tried to sound it out. This stops the reader – the worst thing you can do. (Did the second example above stop you?) You want to stop a reader only when you have written a passage so good that she stops to say, "Wow. That was beautiful." Or terrifying, or poetic, or something else that you were trying to achieve. You never want to stop the reader because she can't figure out what you are saying.

If you need this kind of dialect to set the scene, then use it. But do not continue it throughout the book. You get the idea across to the reader, then ease up. You should try to avoid phonetic spelling, if possible. Elmore Leonard, recognized as a master of dialog, suggests that you use dialect "sparingly."

You can apply this technique when a foreign language is required. In my book *The Silver Medallion, A Crystal Moore Suspense*, a Mexican enters the book. After just a few simple Spanish words that most people can figure out or are made clear by the rest of the conversation, the protagonist pleads with the Mexican to try English. And slowly we transition into all English. The reader now understands that this is a Mexican who has little English, but who is trying. No need to continue to bang the reader with Spanish.

Dialect can add a flavor to your book. Just make sure it is a desirable one. Read how master writers have handled it. Practice it. Listen to what you've written. Get qualified outside readers to check it. Listen to it read aloud. Make it a plus for your book and not a stop sign for the reader.

Exercises

1. Try a short bit of dialog by a character from a wealthy family back in 1920.

2. Try a short piece of dialog by a character from a poor family in 1920.

3. Try a short bit of dialog by a character from a wealthy family in 2021.

4. Try a short piece of dialog by a character from a poor family in 2021.

5. Write a short piece of dialog from a Mexican immigrant who has been in the U.S. for a month.

Chapter 15

Rules of the Road

What do we need to get the mechanics right for dialog? Well, that's easy – this could be a short chapter. We need quotation marks. Simple.

Not so fast. There's a little more to it than that. But, the quotation mark is a good place to start. For simple quotations, we all understand you enclose the actual spoken words within double quotations.

Example: "Stop," he yelled.
She said, "When I feel like it."

Note that the comma and the period both go inside the quotation mark. Earlier I said there were no hard and fast rules in writing. But once we get into the mechanics of writing, there are some rules we need to follow. So, let's get it straight right now.

Rule: Periods and commas go inside the quotation marks. Colons and semicolons generally go outside. Question marks and exclamation marks go inside the last quotation mark if they belong to the quoted matter or both the quoted matter and the rest of the sentence. If they belong only to the rest of the sentence, they go outside the quotation mark.

(These four examples are not dialog. But they illustrate how punctuation is handled with quotation marks.)

Example: This is what Mr. Bilmar listed under "required materials": mosquito repellent, trail mix, rifle. (The colon goes outside the quote mark.)

Example: Who wrote "Cleansed by Fire"? (The question mark is only for the sentence.)

Example: Who wrote "Why Are We Here?" (The question mark is for both the quote and the sentence.)

Example: I heard her scream "Help!" (The exclamation mark is only for the quoted word.)

Rule: Sentences start with a capital letter. Capitalize the first word of a directly quoted sentence even when it appears within another sentence.

Example: Sally said, "It is my desire to remain in this house until I die."

Example: "It is my desire," Sally said, "to remain in this house until I die."

In the first example, *It* is the first word of a sentence, so it is capitalized. In the second example, *to* is not the first word of a sentence, so it is not capitalized.

Full speed ahead and don't spare the paragraphs.

If you have two or more people in a dialog, use a new paragraph and a new set of quotation marks every time the speaker changes.

Example:
"Okay. Let's do it," Jerry said.
Oran shook his head. "I'm not in favor of it."
"Why not?"
"Doesn't feel right."
Jerry frowned. "In what way?"
"I don't know. Something's off."

What if he's long-winded?

If a single speaker says several sentences uninterrupted, enclose them in one set of quotation marks.

Example: "I'd like to go. I deserve to go. Willie wants me to go with him. I can think of no reason why I shouldn't go."

However, if you have a single piece of uninterrupted dialog by one person that extends over several paragraphs, you should start it with an open quote mark. At the end of the paragraph, do not close the quotes. But start the next paragraph with an open quote mark. If the speech extends to other paragraphs, continue this pattern. Do not close the quotes at the end of a paragraph, but do start the next paragraph with a quote. When the speaker finally stops, then – and only then – do you put in the close quotation mark. I found this rule violated in several books I've read lately.

Example:

John stood up. Rose knew right then, he was going to talk for a long time.

"Let me state my position," John started. "I have long been opposed to any change in the way we do things. We have operated with great success over a number of years. I've been here, well, almost since the beginning. I've seen people come and people go. Some have stayed a long time and some only a short time. Some have contributed and some have not.

"Most of you don't remember when we had a fiscal crisis back in, well, I don't remember the exact date. But it was an absolute mess. In fact, I had to step in and try to straighten it out. And I did. And things got back to normal. And that happened without changing the rules, the methods.

"Why mess with success? Why take a chance on ruining a system that has worked and continues to work. Many, many years ago, we formalized the way things should be done. I wrote most of the documentation. It works. Leave it alone."

Rose wasn't disappointed. Actually, she *was* disappointed, but not surprised.

First, I apologize for writing such a long stretch of ... nothing. But, note how the quotation marks are used: an opening quote to start things off, an opening quote to start each paragraph within his speech, and a closing quotation mark when he (finally) finished.

Now, somewhere earlier, I suggested not to have long speeches. I still hold to that. But an occasion may arise where you want a person to make a long speech to illustrate a point about that character, or for some other reason. Fine. But please apply the quotation marks properly. This method tells the reader that it is the same person, still speaking, even though you've gone to another paragraph.

Quotes in quotes

What do you do when a person is speaking and quotes something or someone else? You use double quotes for the person speaking and you enclose the quote the character recites in single quotes.

Example: "The letter said, and I quote, 'Under no circumstances should you reveal the contents of this letter to anyone other than Genovese.' I have not, even though I was tempted." He leaned back and waited for her reaction.

Is it, or isn't it?

If you precede a statement with a word like "that," you do not use quotation marks. The use of "that" makes it indirect discourse and thus deserves no quotations marks.

Example:
Wilfred said, "Johnson agreed to give $100,000 to start the fund."
Wilfred said that Johnson agreed to give $100,000 to start the fund.

The second line is not given as an exact quote. It might be. But it isn't listed as one. The reader doesn't know if Wilfred said, "Johnson agreed to give $100,000 to start the fund," or "Johnson stood up, raised his hands over his head and declared with a flourish, 'I'll get this fund going with an initial bump of one hundred K.' Everybody applauded." It is possible the author didn't want all of Wilfred's statement, so he paraphrased it. No quotes for paraphrasing.

Example: Jack looked at each of us. "Mary said, 'I know who stole the money.' But she didn't tell me who it was."

Example: Jack looked at each of us. "Mary said that she knew who stole the money. But she didn't tell me who it was."

The first "Jack" example above uses a direct quote from Mary within Jack's quote. Note the use of double and single quotation marks. The second "Jack" example uses indirect discourse and hence gets no single quotation marks around the information from Mary.

Example: Jill asked, "Was Jack drunk?"
Jill asked if Jack was drunk.

The second line is indirect discourse, not an exact quote, so we don't put in quotation marks.

However, you *can* use quotations marks if you want to emphasize that you are using someone else's words.

Example: Ben said that "every dollar tucked in a safe is not working."

Internalization

Chapter 8 talked about the importance of internalization. But, it did not have anything to say about the mechanics of incorporating internal dialog into your book. Unfortunately, there is no "Rule" for doing this. The important point here is that you select a method and remain consistent.

First, note that single quotes are *not* an indication of internal dialog. Using single quotes to indicate internalization is a mistake.

What are the methods you can use? Probably the most common method is to put the internal dialog in italics.

Example: Ginnie smiled at the man, but said nothing. *You're out of your mind if you think I'm giving you a book.*

If your use of internalization is light (is not used very much in the book), you can simply state that it is internal dialog.

Example: The woman held a piece of spoiled fruit in her hand. Is that all she has to eat, Lily thought.

If the writer has successfully employed deep POV, it may not be necessary to make any special note of internalization.

Example: Cammie studied the map. I'm lost.

An Important Caveat. Remember, you can employ internalization only for the POV character.

We interrupt this program ...

If you interrupt the dialog of one person briefly, then restart with a quotation mark and remain in the same paragraph.

Example: "Must you hurry off?" She shifted slightly, allowing her silky blouse to slip down, exposing an unblemished shoulder. "You don't want to leave me alone with a nearly full bottle of Merlot, do you?"

On the other hand, if the interruption becomes long, it may be desirable to start a new paragraph when the person continues the dialog. In such a case, a new attribution may be necessary if there is a chance that the reader will not know instantly who is speaking.

Example: Sarah seemed distracted. “I’m not sure why I’m telling you all of this.” She got up and walked to the window, drawing the blinds. Below, she could see people going about their every day chores, or maybe enjoying a vacation. *They’re not worried about having their child kidnapped.* Fear once again invaded her heart. Sarah watched a young boy, about the same age as her Joey, race across the grass, chasing a small black puppy. *Is his mother worried? Does she have anybody she could trust? Do I have anybody I can trust?*

She turned from the window and faced the stranger. “Why should I believe you can help? Why should I trust you?”

In Chapter 11, we discussed a long interruption when two people are in a conversation and the need for attribution when conversation continues. I won’t repeat it here.

We’ve covered a lot of the mechanics of dialog in this chapter. Here are a few exercises to help cement the basics.

Exercises

1. Write a monologue that extends over several paragraphs. (For this exercise, the paragraphs can be very short.) Then, refer back to the section on long monologues and see if you used the quotation marks properly.

2. Make up an example where the question mark goes inside the quotation mark.

3. Make up an example where the question mark should properly be positioned outside the quotation mark.

4. Write a brief example of a quote within a quote, using both single and double quotation marks.

5. Write an example where a short interruption occurs in one person's dialog and use quote marks properly.

6. Write an example where there is a long interruption in one person's dialog. How should this be handled?

7. Write an example using indirect discourse. How are quotes used or not used in this case?

8. Write a brief bit of dialog where the attribution splits the sentence. Check to make certain you have handled capitalization properly.

9. Write a brief bit of dialog that is interrupted by attribution in the middle, and the first part ends with a colon. (If you have trouble coming up with an example, you can punctuate this correctly. "Here is a list of the items you must check Mr. Jones looked at each student. "Capitals, punctuation, spelling split infinitives, quotation marks, and logic.")

Chapter 16

Final Thoughts

Properly, I guess "Final thoughts" should be internalization. But, I'm not doing that. I'm going to share my final thoughts with everyone.

And right off, I'm going to answer the question often posed: Where can I find examples of good dialog? There are many places, but here are a few.

The late Elmore Leonard is considered one of the best on modern dialog, particularly when it comes to the less refined characters. An excellent example is *Get Shorty*. Read the book, don't watch the movie, if you want to learn how to write good dialog. You need to see it in print.

Leonard has his list of ten rules on writing. One is "Never use a verb other than 'said' to carry dialog." Personally, I think "never" is too strong a word. Remember the axiom: Never say never. Another of his rules is: never use an adverb to modify the verb "said."

He also gives his ultimate rule, which he says sums up the ten. "If it sounds like writing, I rewrite it."

Other writers who excel at dialog include Robert B. Parker (most any of the Spenser novels); Tony Morrison (*The Bluest Eye*); here, I'm showing my age, but I want to include James

Thurber (*The Secret Life of Walter Mitty*); and Judy Blume (*Are you there God? It's me, Margaret*).

Of course, it would be hard to go wrong studying John Steinbeck's *Of Mice and Men.* Note the dialog of George and Lennie.

Before you start a section of dialog, decide what you want to accomplish with this piece. What is its purpose? If you cannot state that, and preferably in a short sentence, stop and decide if it is needed at all. If you can state why you need this piece of dialog, it will be easier to write.

Afterwards (this could be soon or after the next chapter is finished), take a look at it and decide if it satisfied its purpose. If you do this consistently, I guarantee your dialog will be better.

Lastly, I want to repeat and elaborate on the advice I tendered earlier. You must read your dialog aloud. You need to think about how you envision the character and how you want the reader to see your character. Does the dialog you have given this character mirror that image? If not, rewrite the dialog until it does.

I know writers who go through a manuscript and read only the words of one character. Is his/her speech consistent? Does it reflect how they want the character to be perceived? Then, they do the same for the next character. This is tedious. But it could be the difference between being well published and not being published at all.

Find a fellow writer whom you think is good. And critical. Read your dialog aloud to this person. How do they react? Do they feel about each character the way you want them to feel?

Have someone else read your dialog aloud while you listen. Do you love it? If you only *like* it, rewrite it. If there isn't any dialog that makes you laugh or cry or makes your heart beat a little faster, you have missed the mark.

Your novel needs a plot. Your novel needs characters. But neither of those will make your novel sing like great dialog.

Exercise

1. Take your latest work. Ask a friend to read the dialog aloud to you. Listen with your eyes closed.

Character: The Heartbeat of the Novel

If you like this book on dialog, you will like Callan's book on character development, ***Character: The Heartbeat of the Novel*** (available in print and digital editions). In it, you will find ways to create memorable characters, the kind of characters that generate great reviews, characters that propel a book into a series.

Some of the topics covered include:

- The importance of selecting names for your characters
- How to sculpt your characters

- Points to consider when creating a character for a series
- The importance of character bios
- Motivation and conflict
- The power of eccentricity
- Creating the *four* dimensional character
- Why you need a strong antagonist
- Points to consider in crafting a sidekick character for the protagonist
- And much more.

Reviews -

"I'm impressed, because it's absolutely the best book I've read so far on character development."
Ginnie Sienna Bivona, former Acquisition Editor and Publisher

"... an easy, enjoyable read with examples and suggested practice exercises. Assembled between the covers of this book are proven ways of bringing the protagonist and antagonist to life as real people the reader will love or despise – and remember long after the novel has been returned to the shelf. He also explains how to develop the perfect sidekick and why this is important."
Galand Nuchols, author of numerous YA and middle grade reader books, including *Dragons for Kris* and *Second Chance.*

About the Author

James R. Callan took a degree in English, intent on writing. But when that did not support a family, he returned to graduate school in the field of mathematics. Upon graduation, he worked as a research mathematician, segueing into computer science, and a thirty year detour from writing.

Along the way, he has received grants from the National Science Foundation, NASA, and the Data Processing Management Association. He has been listed in *Who's Who in America*, *Who's Who in Computer Science*, and *Two Thousand Notable Americans*.

Then one day, he realized his children were grown, self-supporting, and he could return to his original love—writing. For two years, Callan wrote a monthly column for a national magazine. For six months, he wrote a weekly column that appeared in newspapers in four states. Callan has had fourteen books published: five non-fiction books, plus nine mystery/suspense novels. All are presented in both print and digital formats. Eight are also in audio. The audio version of one of his books rose as high as number seven on the publisher's list. He has had shorter works published in five anthologies, and was the editor for another anthology. He also gives workshops in the U.S. and Mexico on various aspects of writing He can be contacted through his website: www.jamesrcallan.com.

He and his wife split their time between homes in east Texas and Puerto Vallarta, Mexico. They have four children and seven grandchildren.

www.ingramcontent.com/pod-product-compliance
Ingram Content Group UK Ltd.
Pitfield, Milton Keynes, MK11 3LW, UK
UKHW041851190726
13854UKWH00002B/830

9 798201 793562